KIDS GET CODING

CODING TO CREATE AND COMMUNICATE

Heather Lyons

Illustrations by Alex Westgate & Dan Crisp

Lerner Publications ◆ Minneapolis

Contents

Children will need access to the Internet for most of the activities in this book. Parents or teachers should supervise Internet use and discuss online safety with children.

Getting Started

Hi, I'm Data Duck! In this book, I will show you the fun and creative things we can do with our computers.

We can use different types of computers to be creative and to communicate—for example phones, tablets, and laptops. We use different programs on these computers to do different things, such as writing an email or calling someone. All programs are written in code, which is a language that computers understand and follow.

DATA DUCK
In this book, we will be using coding blocks. They are sets of code that we can combine to create code for a computer.

There are lots of activities in the book for you to try out. There are also some online activities for you to practice. For the online activities, go to **www.blueshiftcoding.com/ kidsgetcoding** and look for the activity with the page number from the book.

Screen Time

The time we spend in front of a screen is called screen time.
The screen can be our phone, TV, computer, or tablet.
We can spend screen time in four different ways.

1. We use screens to talk to other people or send them messages. This is called communication.

2. Sometimes we use screens to watch TV shows or videos.

3. We use screens to play games.

4. Sometimes we use screens to be creative.

My Screen Time

Think about when you spend time in front of a screen. Write down three things you do during your screen time. Which types of screen time are they?

DATA DUCK
I like to spend my screen time being creative. I write stories, draw pictures, take photographs, and make music.

You Have Mail!

When we talk to someone or send them messages, we are communicating. Using a computer, we can communicate by phoning people, video chatting with them, sending them a text message, or emailing them.

Email stands for "electronic mail." Email is mail that we write and send using computers. When we send an email, it passes to a server. The server sends the email to another server using the Internet. From there, the email is picked up by the right mailbox and reaches the person we sent it to.

DATA DUCK
Servers are huge, very powerful computers that are connected to other computers. When we send an email, servers make sure it travels to the right person through the Internet.

What's Your Address?

Email addresses work a little bit like mailing addresses. They include the name of the person sending and receiving mail and where his or her mailbox is.

This is an email address: dataduck@kidsgetcoding.com
dataduck is the name of the person whose email address this is.
@ means "at" and separates the name of the person from the rest of the address.
kidsgetcoding.com is the domain name of the email address.
Domain names are often owned by companies, the government, or universities.

Data Duck has lots of email addresses! What are the domain names of the companies that own his other mailboxes?

A: dataduck@pondlife.org   B: dataduck@riverside.com

Turn to page 23 to see the answers.

Server sends email
using the Internet

Server receives
email

HOW AN EMAIL TRAVELS

Email travels
to server

Email sent

Email received

Lights, Camera, Action!

Email isn't the only way we can use computers to communicate with our friends and family. We can also get in touch with them by making video calls.

When we make calls using a computer, it works differently than making calls with a regular phone. The computer sends and receives the videos of each caller through the Internet. The video is turned into little packets of information, or data. Once the computer on the other side receives the packets of information, it puts them together and turns them into a picture again.

DATA DUCK

Computers use code to turn something, such as a video, into packets of data before sending it. The code is like an instruction manual. It also tells the computer receiving the packets how to open them and show them as a video.

Being Safe

Look at these questions and pick the answer you think is correct.

When I make a video call, I should:

A. Make sure I'm not hungry

B. Make sure I'm with an adult

C. Bring my teddy

I should only video call people who:

A. I don't know

B. I know and trust

Turn to page 23 to see the answers.

Telling a Story

It is fun to use screen time to be creative. We might draw a picture using our computer or even write a story. To write a story, we need to choose the right program.

A program is a set of code that tells our computer how to do a particular task. Computers have lots of programs, so we need to make sure we choose the right one for each job. If we would like to write a story, we need to use a word processing program.

Your Story

Find out the name of the word processing program on your school's computer or your home computer. Open it and try writing a short story, about four sentences long. Can you find out how to save your story?

DATA DUCK

A word processing program gives us all the tools to write a story. We can type words that will show up on our computer screen, and we can save them, so we don't lose our story.

Sharing Your Work

If you have written a story or a poem, it might be nice to show it to your friends and family. You can use screen time to be creative and share your work using your computer.

In order to share your work safely, always ask a trusted adult to help you. Together, you should think about where you would like to share your story— maybe you know a website that other kids also use? Once you agree on a safe website, you can start the process of uploading your work.

DATA DUCK
We need to be careful about the things we say and the stories and pictures we post on the Internet. Once we upload something, it can be changed and used by anyone else on the Internet too.

Time to Share?

What kinds of things do you think are OK to share on a public website that everyone can see?

A: Your name

B: Your favorite singer's name

C: A photo of yourself

D: Something about your teacher

Turn to page 23 to see the answers.

How to Be Found

Once you have uploaded your work (for example, a picture) to the Internet, it is there for everyone to see! But how will people know it is there, and how can they find it?

The Internet is full of pictures and many other things people like to share. So we need to make sure our picture is easy to find. We can do this by using metadata or tags to describe it. Tags describe a piece of information that we might store on a computer or find on the Internet. When we write a tag with the symbol # at the beginning, we call it a hashtag.

Tags we could use to describe a picture of a beach might be *sand*, *beach*, *sun*, and *palm tree*.

DATA DUCK
You can search the Internet using a website called a search engine. One search engine, for example, is Google. We type words that describe what we are looking for into a search engine. Then the search engine looks for metadata that matches those words.

Tag It!

Carefully look at a picture. What does it show?
Write down at least five words that describe the picture. These are your tags, or metadata!

Say "Cheese!"

One of the really clever and creative things we can do with a computer is take photos! But how does this work? And what else can we do with our pictures once we have taken them?

After we have taken a picture, our computer turns this picture into millions of little squares, which we call pixels. Each pixel can then be described using numbers.

The numbers tell us where the pixel is in the picture. This is helpful when we would like to tell our computer to change our photo in some way.

DATA DUCK
The opposite page shows what a picture might look like when a computer saves it. The black lines are called a grid. When we describe where a pixel is, we use the grid labels "horizontal position" and "vertical position," and say how far along the pixel is on each of these sides of the grid. These are the pixel's coordinates.

Color Change

Look at the picture below and imagine you want to tell your computer to change the color of the big red square. Can you describe to your computer where each pixel is that needs to be changed? Write down the coordinates of each pixel on a piece of paper.

Turn to page 23 to see the answers.

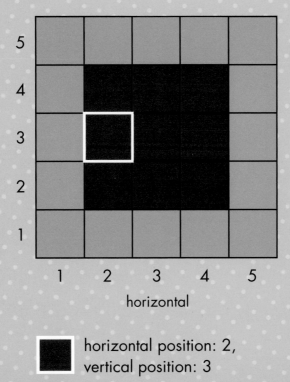

vertical

5

4

3

2

1

1   2   3   4   5

horizontal

horizontal position: 2,
vertical position: 3

Drum Roll, Please!

Did you know that you can use your computer to make music? Using the right program, you can get creative and write whole songs on a laptop, a tablet, or even a phone!

The way our computer understands music is a little like the way it understands pictures: it uses letters. Using a music program, each note is changed to a number before it is stored on a computer. The numbers are a kind of code that tell the computer how to play the piece of music.

Old MacDonald had a farm
C C C G A A G

E – I – E – I – O
E E D D C

Let's Code Music!

Look at the musical notes for the song *Old MacDonald*, on the opposite page. We have already coded the first line *(below left)*. Can you arrange the coding blocks below right in the correct order, so a computer can play the second line?

Turn to page 23 to see the answers.

DATA DUCK

When we write down music on paper, we use a language like code too. It's called musical notation, and it is able to tell us which notes to play, for how long, and how loudly.

Repeat 2 times

Repeat 3 times

Play note C (60)

Repeat 2 times

Play note G (55)

Repeat 2 times

Play note A (57)

Play note D (62)

Play note C (60)

Play note G (55)

Play note E (64)

Exploring the Internet

Sometimes we need to find out information before we can create things. We can use a computer to find out information about anything from animals to Olympic sports by using the Internet. But it is helpful to follow a few rules . . .

If you want to do research on the Internet, you should always do this with an adult you trust. The Internet is full of exciting and amazing facts, but it can be hard to find them. An adult can help you choose the right websites and teach you how to explore the Internet safely and quickly.

DATA DUCK

The Internet can be a great place to go if you need to do research for a school project, for example. But it is important to use websites that give us the right information. To make sure the information we have found is correct, we can either check other websites or ask an adult.

True or Not?

When we use the Internet to find out information, we need to know how to make sure that it's correct.

A: Data Duck reads an article about ostriches in space on a website. Would you trust the information on this website? Why?

B: On one website, Data Duck reads that his favorite football player is changing teams, but three other websites say he's not. Do you think this information is true or false? Why?

Turn to page 23 to see the answers.

Extension Activities

Go to **blueshiftcoding.com/kidsgetcoding** for more fun activities and to practice:

- using coding blocks
- writing programs
- predicting what programs will do
- coding music
- changing the color of pixels

Words to Remember

code: the arrangement of instructions in a computer program

coordinates: letters and numbers used together to describe a position

email: mail that is sent electronically, with the help of computers

Internet: a giant network of computers that are all connected together

pixel: a tiny square on a computer screen. Computers save pictures by turning them into millions of tiny pixels.

server: a huge computer that is connected to other computers

Activity Answers

p. 7
The domain names of Data Duck's other email addresses are:

A: pondlife.com

B: riverside.com

p. 9
When I make a video call, I should:

B. Make sure I'm with an adult

I should only video call people who:

B. I know and trust

p. 13
B. It's OK to share your favorite singer's name.

Remember, you should share as little as possible about yourself and other people on public websites because everyone can see it. Never share your name and address or anything about your teachers or school, and never upload any pictures of yourself or others.

p. 17
The positions of the pixels that need changing are:

horizontal position: 4, vertical position: 2
horizontal position: 4, vertical position: 3
horizontal position: 4, vertical position: 4
horizontal position: 3, vertical position: 2
horizontal position: 3, vertical position: 3
horizontal position: 3, vertical position: 4
horizontal position: 2, vertical position: 2
horizontal position: 2, vertical position: 3
horizontal position: 2, vertical position: 4

p. 19

```
Repeat 2 times
    Play note E (64)

Repeat 2 times
    Play note D (62)

Play note C (60)
```

p. 21
A: Based on what you have learned in school, you probably know that there aren't any ostriches in space. If you can figure out for yourself that something on a website is wrong, it's best not to use it for any other information either.

B: If three websites say something different from the one you're checking, it's likely that the website you're looking at isn't giving you the right information.

Index

First American edition published in 2018 by Lerner Publishing Group, Inc.
First published in Great Britain in 2017 by Wayland, an imprint of Hachette Children's Group
Copyright © Hodder & Stoughton, 2017
Text copyright © Heather Lyons

Lerner Publications Company
A division of Lerner Publishing Group, Inc.
241 First Avenue North
Minneapolis, MN 55401 USA

For reading levels and more information, look up this title at www.lernerbooks.com.

Main body text set in Futura Std. Book 12/16. Typeface provided by Adobe Systems.

Library of Congress Cataloging-in-Publication Data
Names: Lyons, Heather (Heather K.), author. | Westgate, Alex, illustrator. | Crisp, Dan, illustrator. | Lyons, Heather (Heather K.). Kids get coding.
Title: Coding to create and communicate / Heather Lyons ; illustrated by Alex Westgate and Dan Crisp.
Description: Minneapolis : Lerner Publications, [2018] | Series: Kids get coding | Audience: Ages 6–10. | Audience: K to grade 3. | Includes bibliographical references and index.
Identifiers: LCCN 2016056355 (print) | LCCN 2017000028 (ebook) | ISBN 9781512439441 (lb : alk. paper) | ISBN 9781512455847 (pb : alk. paper) | ISBN 9781512450521 (eb pdf)
Subjects: LCSH: Computer programming—Juvenile literature. | Telecommunication—Juvenile literature.
Classification: LCC QA76.6 .L88527 2018 (print) | LCC QA76.6 (ebook) | DDC 005.1—dc23

LC record available at https://lccn.loc.gov/2016056355

Printed in China